Ninja Dual Zone 2023 Air Fryer Cookbook with Pictures

Quick & Tasty Ninja Foodi Dual Zone Air Fryer AF300UK Recipes For Beginners & advanced

UK 2500

By: Gabriel Andrews

TABLE OF CONTENTS

BREAKFAST

Banana Oatmeal Recipe..................................1

Dates Millet Pudding.................................... 2

Potatoes with lamb..3

Air Fried Sandwich..4

Mushroom Oatmeal.......................................5

Pea Tortilla.. 6

Cheesy Sandwich...7

Delicious Creamy Eggs................................. 8

Mushroom Quiches....................................... 9

FISH AND SEAFOOD

Salmon and Greek Yogurt Sauce...............10

Air Fried Cod...11

Mouthwatering Cod with Plum Sauce.......12

Tilapia & Chives Sauce..................................13

Tasty Catfish...14

Stuffed Calamari Recipe..............................15

Chinese Style Cod..16

Hawaiian Salmon Recipe............................17

Catfish Fillets Recipe...................................18

POULTRY RECIPES

Turkey Quarters and Veggies.......................19

Chicken and Garlic Sauce.........................20

Chicken Breasts & Tomatoes Sauce.......... 21

Duck Breasts Recipe................................ 22

Chicken Thighs and Baby Potatoes.......... 23

Chicken and Apricot Sauce Recipe..........24

Duck and Veggies Recipe............................25

Chicken & Simple Coconut Sauce.............26

Chicken Breasts & BBQ Chilli Sauce..........27

MAIN RECIPES

Special Sausage 28

Veggie Toasts 29

Mouthwatering chicken Sandwiches 30

Chicken Wings 31

Special Seafood Stew 32

Beef Garlic Pizzas 33

Tasty Hash Brown Toasts 34

Cheese Burgers 35

Japanese Style Chicken 36

MEAT RECIPES

Garlic Lamb Chops Recipe........................ 37

Beef Brisket and Onion Sauce................... 38

Beef Patties & Mushroom Sauce................ 39

Beef Stuffed Squash Recipe...................... 40

Beef & Green Onions Marinade................. 41

Beef Curry Recipe.................................... 42

Sirloin Steaks & Pico De Gallo................... 43

Balsamic Beef Recipe............................... 44

Beef Casserole Recipe.............................. 45

SIDES RECIPES

Fried Creamy Cabbage..............................46

Brussels Sprouts Dish..............................47

Brussels Sprouts & Pomegranate................48

Onion Rings Dish..............................49

Mushrooms and Cream..............................50

Roasted Peppers Dish..............................51

Delicious Cauliflower Cakes.....................52

Beet Fries Dish..............................53

Pumpkin Rice Dish..............................54

VEGETABLE RECIPES

Simple Tomatoes & Red Pepper Sauce... 55

Mexican Peppers Recipe..56

Asian Potatoes Recipe..57

Green Beans and Parmesan....................... 58

Broccoli Hash Recipe.................................. 59

Broccoli Salad Recipe................................. 60

Peppers Stuffed with Beef........................... 61

Potatoes and Special Tomato Sauce....... 62

Stuffed Poblano Peppers............................63

STARTERS RECIPES

Herbed Tomatoes.. 64

Chestnut and Shrimp Rolls.................................... 65

Tasty Crab Sticks... 66

Tasty Fish Sticks.. 67

Mouthwatering Beef Rolls..................................... 68

Delicious Shrimp Muffins...................................... 69

Quick Courgette Cakes.. 70

Tasty Stuffed Peppers.. 71

Tasty Apple Chips... 72

DESSERT RECIPES

Pumpkin Pie Recipe.. 73

Black Tea Cake.. 74

Mini Lava Cakes Recipe.. 75

Special Brownies Recipe.. 76

Lentils and Dates Brownies...................................... 77

Cocoa Cake Recipe.. 78

Sponge Cake Recipe.. 79

Banana Cake Recipe.. 80

Plum Cake Recipe.. 81

Banana Oatmeal Recipe

Time: 30 Minutes

Servings: 8

Ingredients

- 1 banana; peeled and mashed
- 500g rolled oats
- 80g Light brown sugar
- 5g baking powder
- 160g blueberries
- 125g chocolate chips
- 500ml milk
- 1 egg
- 30g butter
- 5g cinnamon powder
- 5ml vanilla extract
- Cooking spray

Directions:

1. Combine the baking powder with sugar, cinnamon, blueberries, chocolate chips and banana in a medium bowl and stir.
2. Combine the eggs, vanilla extract and butter in another bowl and stir.
3. Heat up your Ninja Dual Zone Air Fryer at 70 degrees C; grease the drawer with cooking spray, Select BAKE and add oats on the bottom.
4. Add the first mixture then the second; toss and cook for twenty mins. Stir another time, transfer to serving bowls and serve for breakfast.

Dates Millet Pudding

Time: 25 Minutes

Servings: 4

Ingredients

- 400ml milk
- 160g millet
- 4 dates; pitted
- 200ml water
- Honey for serving

Directions:

1. Place the millet into a pan that matches your Ninja Dual Zone Air Fryer; add dates, milk, and water; stir.
2. Introduce the pan to the drawer, and insert the drawer onto the Ninja Dual Zone Air Fryer.
3. Choose the BAKE mode and cook at 180°C, for fifteen mins. Divide among plates; drizzle honey on top and serve as breakfast.

Potatoes with Lamb

Time: 30 Minutes

Servings: 4

Ingredients

- 4 potatoes; peeled and cut into medium cubes
- 6 garlic cloves; minced
- 15ml olive oil
- 2 eggs; whisked
- 2 rosemary springs; chopped.
- 4 lamb slices; chopped.
- Salt and black pepper to the taste

Directions:

1. Place potatoes in a pan that fits the drawer of your Ninja Dual Zone Air Fryer and combine them with oil, garlic, lamb, rosemary, salt, pepper, and eggs and whisk.
2. Select ROAST and Cook at 200°C, for twenty mins; transfer to your serving plates and serve as breakfast.

Air Fried Sandwich

Time: 16 Minutes

Servings: 2

Ingredients

- 2 beef strips
- 2 eggs
- 2 English muffins; halved
- Salt and black pepper to the taste

Directions:

1. Crack eggs in the drawer of the Ninja Dual Zone Air Fryer, add beef on top; Select AIR FRY mode, cover and cook at 200ºC, for six mins.
2. Preheat the muffin halves in your microwave for a bit; separate eggs into two halves, add beef on top, season with salt and pepper; cover with the other two English muffins and serve as breakfast.

Mushroom Oatmeal

Time: 30 Minutes
Servings: 4

Ingredients

- 1 small yellow onion; chopped.
- 125g gouda cheese; grated
- 125ml water
- 250g steel-cut oats
- 2 garlic cloves; minced
- 30g butter
- 400ml canned chicken stock
- 3 thyme springs; chopped.
- 30ml extra-virgin olive oil
- 225g mushroom; sliced
- Salt and black pepper to the taste

Directions:

1. Preheat a pan that matches the drawer of your Ninja Dual Zone Air Fryer with the butter over medium heat, add garlic and onions; stir and cook for four mins.
2. Now add oats, water, salt, pepper, stock and thyme; stir, place the an into the drawer, insert the drawer in the Ninja Dual Zone Air Fryer and cook on the AIR FRY mode at 180ºC, for sixty mins.
3. Meantime; preheat a pan with the olive oil over medium heat, add mushrooms, and cook them for three mins; add to oatmeal and cheese; stir, transfer to serving bowls and serve as breakfast.

Pea Tortilla

Time: 17 Minutes

Servings: 8

Ingredients

- Eight eggs
- 60g butter
- 225g baby peas
- 680g yoghurt
- 125g mint; chopped.
- Salt and black pepper

Directions:

1. Preheat a pan that matches your Ninja air fryer drawer with the butter over medium heat, add peas; stir and cook for a couple of minutes.
2. Meantime; combine 1/2 of the yoghurt with salt, pepper, eggs and mint in a bowl and whisk well.
3. Pour the mixture over the peas, toss, place the pan into the drawer, insert the drawer in your Ninja dua zone air fryer, select BAKE and cook at 175ºC, for seven mins. Spread the rest of the yoghurt over your tortilla; slice and serve.

Cheesy Sandwich

Time: 18 Minutes

Servings: 1

Ingredients

- Two bread slices
- Two cheddar cheese slices
- 10g butter
- A pinch of sweet paprika

Directions:

1. Spread butter on the bread slices, add cheddar cheese on one, sprinkle paprika, top with the other bread slices, and cut into two halves.
2. Arrange them in your Ninja dual zone air fryer, Select AIR FRY and cook at 187°C, for eight mins; flipping them once, place them on a platter and serve.

Delicious Creamy Eggs

Time: 18 Minutes

Servings: 1

Ingredients

- Four eggs
- 10g chives; chopped.
- 30g Double cream
- Two beef ham slices
- 45g parmesan; grated
- 10g butter; soft
- Salt and black pepper to the taste
- A pinch of smoked paprika

Directions:

1. Grease a pan that matches the drawer of your Ninja Dual Zone Air Fryer with butter; line it with the beef ham and add it to your air fryer's basket.
2. Combine one egg with Double cream, salt and pepper in a bowl whisk well and add the whole mixture over the beef ham.
3. Crack the remaining eggs in the pan, sprinkle parmesan, Choose BAKE and cook your mix for twelve mins at 160 degrees C. Sprinkle paprika and chives all over; transfer to plates and serve as breakfast.

Mushroom Quiches

Time: 18 Minutes
Servings: 1

Ingredients

- Two chopped button mushrooms
- A chopped small yellow onion
- 30g chopped beef ham
- 3g thyme; dried
- 60g Swiss cheese; grated
- 80g Double cream
- Three eggs
- 15g flour
- 15g butter; soft
- 9-inch pie dough
- A pinch of nutmeg; ground
- Salt and black pepper

Directions:

1. Dust your working board with the flour and roll the pie dough on it, then put it in the bottom of a pie pan that matches the drawer of your Ninja Dual Zone Air Fryer and press.
2. Combine butter with mushrooms, beef ham, eggs, onion, Double cream, salt & pepper, thyme and nutmeg in a bowl and whisk well
3. Pour this mixture over the pie crust in the pan, spread, sprinkle Swiss cheese on top and place the pan in the drawer, insert the drawer into the Ninja Dual Zone Air Fryer.
4. Select BAKE and cook at 200ºC, for ten mins. Slice and serve as breakfast.

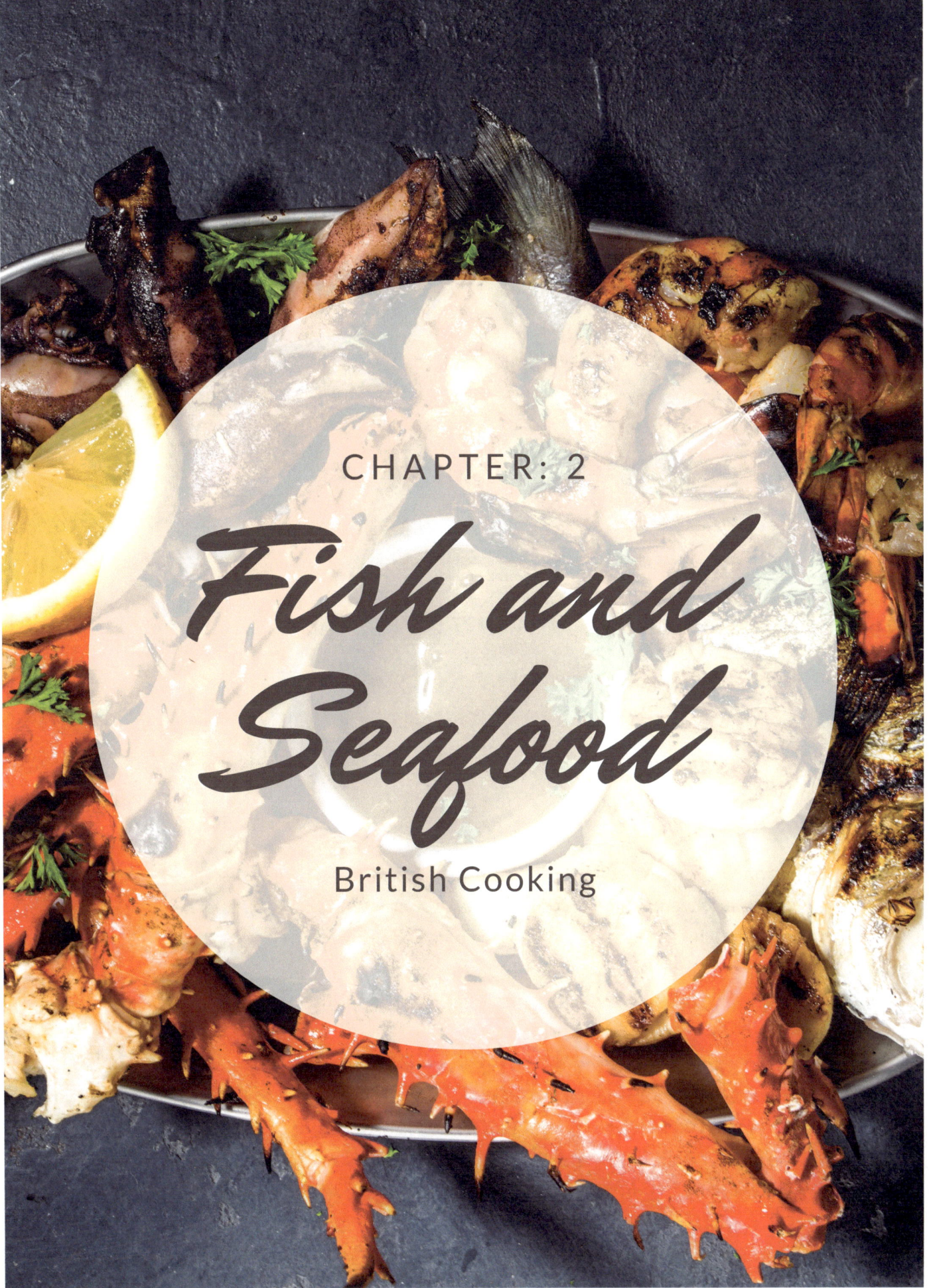

CHAPTER: 2
Fish and Seafood
British Cooking

Salmon and Greek Yogurt Sauce

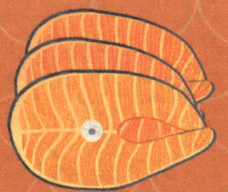

Time: 25 Minutes

Servings: 4

Ingredients

- Two medium salmon fillets
- 15g chopped basil
- 250g Greek yoghurt
- Six lemon slices
- 3g mint; chopped.
- 3g Coriander; chopped.
- 10g curry powder
- A pinch of cayenne pepper
- A minced garlic clove
- Sea salt and black pepper

Directions:

1. Put each salmon fillet on a parchment paper piece, make three splits in each, stuff them with basil and season with salt & pepper.
2. Top each fillet with three slices of lemon, fold the parchment, and seal the edges.
3. Place them in the drawers of your Ninja Dual Zone Air Fryer, insert them into the unit and set zone 1 to BAKE at 200ºC and set the time to twenty mins. Select the "MATCH" choice to apply the settings of the first zone to the second zone. Then press START/STOP to start.
4. Meantime; in a bowl, mix yoghurt with cayenne pepper, salt to the taste, garlic, curry, mint and Coriander and whisk well.
5. Place the fish in platters, drizzle the yoghurt sauce you've just prepared on top and serve immediately!

Air Fried Cod

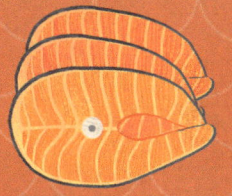

Time: 22 Minutes

Servings: 4

Ingredients

- Two codfish; 7-ounce each
- 5ml dark soy sauce
- 60ml light soy sauce
- 45ml olive oil
- 15g sugar
- 4 ginger slices
- 3 spring onions; chopped.
- 15g coriander; chopped.
- 250ml water
- A drizzle of sesame oil
- Salt and black pepper

Directions:

1. Season fish with salt, and pepper, drizzle sesame oil, rub well and leave aside for ten mins.
2. Place the codfish in both drawers of your Ninja Dual Zone Air Fryer, insert them into the unit and set zone 1 to AIR FRY at 180ºC and set the time to twelve mins. Select the "MATCH" choice to apply the settings of the first zone to the second zone. Then press START/STOP to start.
3. Meantime; heat up a pot with the water over medium heat, add dark and light soy sauce and sugar; stir, bring to a simmer and take off the heat.
4. Preheat a pan with the olive oil over medium heat, add ginger and green onions; stir, cook for a few minutes and take off the heat. transfer the cooked fish to serving plates, top with ginger and green onions, drizzle soy sauce mix, sprinkle coriander, and serve immediately.

Mouthwatering Cod Steaks with Plum Sauce

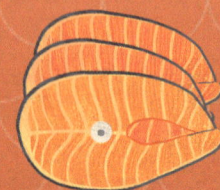

Time: 30 Minutes

Servings: 2

Ingredients

- Two big cod steaks
- 3g garlic powder
- 15ml plum sauce
- 1g turmeric powder
- 3g ginger powder
- Salt and black pepper
- Cooking spray

Directions:

1. Season cod steaks with salt and pepper, spray them with cooking oil, add garlic powder, ginger powder and turmeric powder, and rub well.
2. Place cod steaks in the drawer of your Ninja Dual Zone Air Fryer, Select AIR FRY and cook at 180°C, for fifteen mins; flipping them after seven mins.
3. Preheat a pan over medium heat, add plum sauce; stir and cook for two mins. Divide cod steaks on plates, drizzle the plum sauce on top and serve.

Tilapia & Chives Sauce

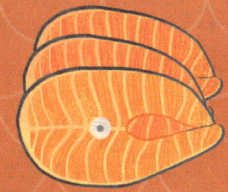

Time: 18 Minutes

Servings: 4

Ingredients

- Four medium tilapia fillets
- 60g Greek yoghurt
- 30g chives; chopped.
- 10g honey
- Juice from 1 lemon
- Cooking spray
- Salt and black pepper

Directions:

1. Season fish with salt and pepper, spray with cooking spray and place in the drawers of your the preheated Ninja Dual Zone Air Fryer.
2. Insert both drawers into the unit, set zone 1 to AIR FRY at 175ºC and set the time to eight mins. Select the "MATCH" choice to apply the settings of the first zone to the second zone. Then press START/STOP to start; flipping halfway.
3. Meanwhile; in a bowl, mix yoghurt with honey, salt, pepper, chives, and lemon juice and whisk well.
4. Transfer the cooked fish to serving plates, drizzle yoghurt sauce all over, and serve immediately.

Tasty Catfish

Time: 30 Minutes
Servings: 4

Ingredients

- Four catfish fillets
- 15ml lemon juice
- 15g parsley; chopped.
- 15ml olive oil
- A pinch of sweet paprika
- Salt and black pepper

Directions:

1. Season catfish fillets with salt, pepper, and paprika, drizzle oil, rub well and arrange them in the drawers of your the preheated Ninja Dual Zone Air Fryer.
2. Insert both drawers into the unit, set zone 1 to AIR FRY at 200°C and set the time to twenty mins. Select the "MATCH" choice to apply the settings of the first zone to the second zone. Then press START/STOP to start; flipping after ten mins.
3. Transfer the fish to serving plates, drizzle lemon juice on top, add parsley over and serve.

Stuffed Calamari Recipe

Time: 35 Minutes

Servings: 4

Ingredients

- Four big calamari; tentacles separated and chopped and tubes reserved
- 30g parsley; chopped.
- 60g canned tomato puree
- 140g kale; chopped.
- Two minced garlic cloves
- A chopped red pepper
- 15ml olive oil
- A chopped yellow onion
- Salt and black pepper

Directions:

1. Preheat a pan with the oil over medium heat; add onion and garlic; stir and cook for two mins.
2. Add red pepper, calamari tentacles, tomato puree, kale, salt and pepper; stir, cook for ten mins and take off the heat. stir and cook for three mins.
3. Install the crisper plates, and put half of the tubes into the first and half into the second drawer of your Ninja Dual Zone Air Fryer.
4. Set zone 1 to AIR FRY at 180°C and set the time to twenty mins.
5. Select the "MATCH" choice to apply the settings of the first zone to the second zone. Then press START/STOP to start.
6. Transfer to serving platters; sprinkle parsley on top and serve.

Chinese Style Cod

Time: 20 Minutes

Servings: 2

Ingredients

- Two boneless medium cod fillets
- 3g ginger; grated
- 5g peanuts; crushed
- 15ml light soy sauce
- 10g garlic powder

Directions:

1. Put fish fillets in a heatproof dish that matches the drawer of your Ninja Dual Zone Air Fryer, add garlic powder, soy sauce, and ginger; toss well, put it in the drawer and insert it into the unit.
2. Select AIR FRY and cook at 175ºC, for ten mins. Transfer to serving plates, sprinkle peanuts on top and serve.

Hawaiian Salmon Recipe

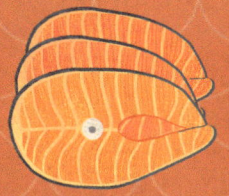

Time: 20 Minutes

Servings: 2

Ingredients

- 560g canned pineapple pieces and juice
- 10g garlic powder
- Two boneless medium salmon fillets
- 5g onion powder
- 15ml balsamic vinegar
- 3g ginger; grated
- Salt and black pepper

Directions:

1. Season salmon with garlic powder, onion powder, salt, and black pepper, rub well, transfer to a heatproof dish that matches the drawer of your Ninja Dual Zone Air Fryer, add ginger and pineapple chunks and toss gently.
2. Drizzle the vinegar over, place it in the drawer and insert it into the unit.
3. Select AIR FRY and cook at 175°C, for ten mins. Transfer to serving plates and serve.

Catfish Fillets Recipe

Time: 22 Minutes
Servings: 4

Ingredients

- Two catfish fillets
- 3g jerk seasoning
- 180g catsup
- 3g garlic; minced
- 5g mustard
- 15ml balsamic vinegar
- 15g parsley; chopped.
- 110ml Worcestershire sauce
- 60g butter
- Salt and black pepper

Directions:

1. Preheat a pan with the butter over medium heat, add Worcestershire sauce, mustard, jerk seasoning, garlic, catsup, vinegar, salt, and pepper; stir well, take off the heat and add fish fillets.
2. Toss well, leave aside for ten mins; drain fillets, place them in both drawers, and insert the drawers into them to your preheated Ninja Dual Zone Air Fryer.
3. Set zone 1 to AIR FRY at 175ºC and set the time to eight mins.
4. Select the "MATCH" choice to apply the settings of the first zone to the second zone. Then press START/STOP to start; flipping fillets halfway.
5. Transfer to serving plates, sprinkle parsley over and serve immediately.

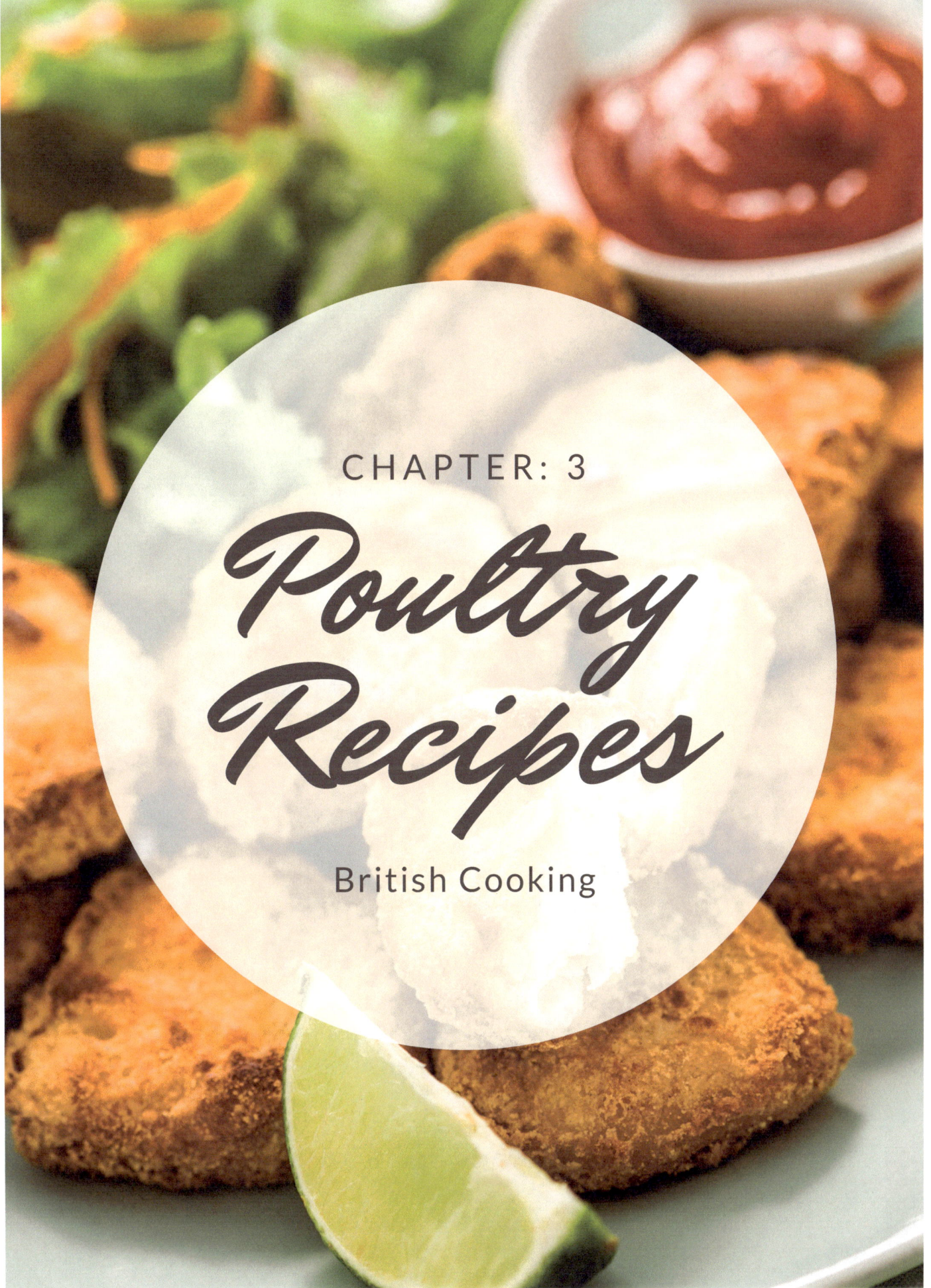

CHAPTER: 3

Poultry Recipes

British Cooking

Turkey Quarters and Veggies

Time: 44 Minutes

Servings: 4

Ingredients

- 3g rosemary; dried
- 3g sage; dried
- 3g thyme; dried
- A chopped yellow onion
- A chopped carrot
- Three minced garlic cloves
- 900g turkey quarters
- A chopped celery stalk
- 250ml chicken stock
- 30ml olive oil
- Two bay leaves
- Salt and black pepper

Directions:

1. Rub turkey quarters with salt, pepper, half of the oil, thyme, sage, rosemary, and thyme, and place them in the drawer of your Ninja Dual Zone Air Fryer.
2. Insert the drawer into the unit, Select ROAST and cook at 180ºC, for twenty mins.
3. In a pan that matches the drawer of your Ninja Dual Zone Air Fryer, combine the carrot with onion, garlic, the rest of the oil, celery, stock, bay leaves, salt and pepper, and toss.
4. Add the turkey, place the pan inside the drawer and cook at 180ºC, for an additional fourteen mins. Transfer to plates and serve.

Chicken and Garlic Sauce

Time: 30 Minutes

Servings: 4

Ingredients

- Four chicken breasts; skin on and bone-in
- 40 garlic cloves; peeled and chopped.
- 15g butter; melted
- 15ml olive oil
- Two thyme sprigs
- 60ml chicken stock
- 30g parsley; chopped.
- Salt and black pepper
- 60ml Apple Cider Vinegar

Directions:

1. Season chicken breasts with salt and pepper, rub with the oil, place in your Ninja Dual Zone Air Fryer, choose AIR FRY and cook at 180ºC, for four mins on each side and place in a heatproof dish that matches the drawer of your Ninja Dual Zone Air Fryer.
2. Add melted butter, garlic, thyme, stock, Apple cider vinegar, and parsley; toss, put in the drawer, insert the drawer into the Ninja Air Fryer, select AIR FRY and cook at 175ºC, for an additional fifteen mins. Transfer to your serving plates and serve.

Chicken Breasts & Tomatoes Sauce

Time: 30 Minutes

Servings: 4

Ingredients

- Four chicken breasts; skinless and boneless
- 390g chopped canned tomatoes
- 1g garlic powder
- 60ml balsamic vinegar
- 60g parmesan; grated
- Salt and black pepper
- A chopped red onion
- Cooking spray

Directions:

1. Spray a baking dish that matches the drawer of your Ninja Dual Zone Air Fryer with cooking oil, add chicken, and season with salt & pepper, garlic powder, balsamic vinegar, tomatoes and cheese; toss.
2. Put in the drawer, insert the drawer into the Ninja Air Fryer, select AIR FRY and cook at 200ºC, for twenty mins. Transfer to your serving plates and serve.

Duck Breasts Recipe

Time: 50 Minutes

Servings: 6

Ingredients

- Six halved duck breasts
- 45g flour
- 90g butter; melted
- 500g mushrooms; chopped.
- 500ml chicken stock
- 60g parsley; chopped.
- Salt and black pepper

Directions:

1. Season duck breasts with salt and pepper, place them in a bowl, add melted butter; toss and transfer to another bowl.
2. Mix flour with melted butter, salt & pepper, and chicken stock and stir well.
3. Arrange duck breasts in a baking dish that matches the drawer of your Ninja Dual Zone Air Fryer, pour the sauce over them, and add parsley along with mushrooms.
4. Put in the drawer, insert the drawer into the Ninja Air Fryer, select AIR FRY and cook at 175°C, for forty mins. Transfer to your serving plates and serve.

Chicken Thighs and Baby Potatoes

Time: 40 Minutes

Servings: 4

Ingredients

- Eight chicken thighs
- 450g halved baby potatoes
- 30ml olive oil
- 10g rosemary; dried
- 10g thyme; chopped.
- 10g oregano; dried
- Two garlic cloves; minced
- A chopped red onion
- 3g sweet paprika
- Salt and black pepper

Directions:

1. Combine chicken thighs with potatoes, garlic, salt & pepper, paprika, onion, rosemary, thyme, oregano and oil in a large bowl.
2. Toss to coat, and spread everything in a heat-proof dish that matches the drawer of your Ninja Dual Zone Air Fryer.
3. Put in the drawer, insert the drawer into the Ninja Air Fryer, select ROAST and cook at 200ºC, for thirty mins; shaking halfway. Transfer to your serving plates and serve.

Chicken and Apricot Sauce Recipe

Time: 30 Minutes

Servings: 4

Ingredients

- A whole chicken; cut into medium pieces
- 30g honey
- 3g marjoram; dried
- 3g smoked paprika
- 60ml water
- 30ml white vinegar
- 15ml olive oil
- 60g apricot preserves
- 8g ginger; grated
- 60ml chicken stock
- Salt and black pepper

Directions:

1. Use some salt & pepper with marjoram, and paprika to season the chicken; toss to coat, add oil, rub well, place the drawer of your Ninja Dual Zone Air Fryer, Select AIR FRY and cook at 180ºC, for ten mins.
2. Now place the chicken in a pan that matches the drawer of your Ninja Dual Zone Air Fryer, add water, stock, ginger, vinegar, apricot preserves and honey; toss.
3. Put in the drawer, insert the drawer into the unit, select ROAST and cook at 180ºC, for an additional ten mins. Transfer the combine to your serving plates and serve.

Duck and Veggies Recipe

Time: 30 Minutes

Servings: 8

Ingredients

- A whole duck; chopped into medium pieces
- 250ml chicken stock
- Two chopped carrots
- A grated small ginger piece
- Three chopped cucumbers
- 45ml water
- Salt and black pepper

Directions:

1. In a pan that matches the drawer of your Ninja Dual Zone Air Fryer, combine the duck pieces with cucumbers, water, carrots, ginger, stock, salt, and pepper; toss, insert the drawer into the unit and cook at 187°C, for twenty mins. Transfer to your serving plates and serve.

Chicken & Simple Coconut Sauce

Time: 22 Minutes

Servings: 6

Ingredients

- 1.36kg chicken breasts
- 250ml chicken stock
- 300g of chopped yellow onion
- 15ml lime juice
- 5g red pepper flakes
- 30g green onions; chopped.
- 15ml olive oil
- 60ml coconut milk
- 10g sweet paprika
- Salt and black pepper

Directions:

1. Preheat a pan that matches the drawer of your Ninja Dual Zone Air Fryer with the oil over medium-high heat, add onions; stir and cook for four mins.
2. Add coconut milk along with stock, pepper flakes, paprika, lime juice, salt & pepper and stir well.
3. Now add the chicken to this mix in the pan, season with some additional salt & pepper; toss.
4. Place the pan in the drawer, insert the drawer into the Ninja Air Fryer, select BAKE and cook at 180ºC, for twelve mins. Transfer to your serving plates and serve.

Chicken Breasts & BBQ Chilli Sauce

Time: 30 Minutes

Servings: 6

Ingredients

- Six skinless and boneless chicken breasts
- 500g ketchup
- 250g pear jelly
- 500g chilli sauce
- 5g garlic powder
- 60g honey
- 3g liquid smoke
- 5g chilli powder
- 5g mustard powder
- 5g sweet paprika
- Salt and black pepper

Directions:

1. Use some salt & pepper to season the breasts, divide them between the drawers of your preheated Ninja Dual Zone Air Fryer, Insert both drawers into the unit, set zone 1 to AIR FRY at 175°C and set the time to ten mins. Select the "MATCH" choice to apply the settings of the first zone to the second zone. Then press START/STOP to start.
2. Meantime; preheat a pan with the chilli sauce over medium heat, add honey, ketchup, liquid smoke, pear jelly, chilli powder, powder, sweet paprika, mustard, salt & pepper and the garlic powder; stir, then turn the heat to simmer and cook for ten mins.
3. Add the pre-cooked breasts; toss to coat, transfer to your serving plates and serve.

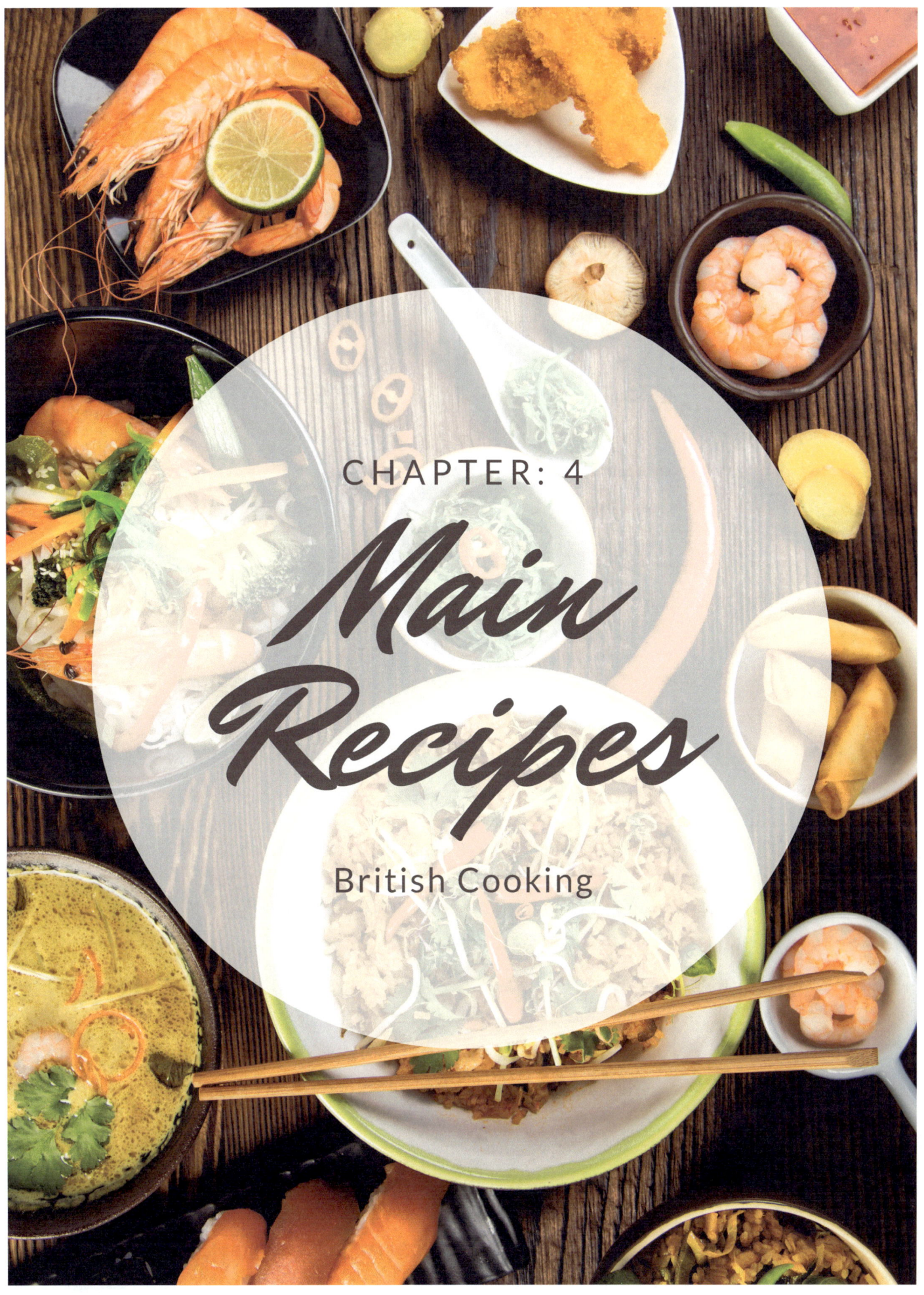

CHAPTER: 4

Main Recipes

British Cooking

Special Sausage

Time: 20 Minutes

Servings: 4

Ingredients

- 450g sausages; sliced
- 80g ketchup
- 125g yellow onion; chopped.
- 125ml chicken stock
- 45g Light brown sugar
- 30g mustard
- A red pepper; cut into strips
- 30ml apple cider vinegar

Directions:

1. Combine ketchup with sugar, mustard, stock, and vinegar in a bowl and whisk well.
2. Combine the sausage slices with red pepper, onion, and sweet and sour mix in the drawer of your Ninja Dual Zone Air Fryer; toss.
3. Insert the drawer into the unit, Select AIR FRY and cook at 175ºC, for ten mins. Transfer to your serving plates and serve.

Veggie Toasts

Time: 25 Minutes

Servings: 4

Ingredients

- A red pepper; cut into thin strips
- 250g sliced cremini mushrooms
- Two sliced green onions
- 15ml olive oil
- 30g soft butter
- Four bread slices
- A chopped yellow squash
- 125g crumbled goat cheese

Directions:

1. Combine red pepper & mushrooms, green onions, squash and oil in a bowl, and toss; transfer to the drawer of your Ninja Dual Zone Air Fryer, Select ROAST and cook them at 175°C, for ten mins; shake the drawer once and place the combine in a bowl.
2. Spread butter on bread slices; arrange them in the drawer of your Ninja Dual Zone Air Fryer and roast them at 175°C, for five mins. Add the veggie combine to the bread slices, add crumbled cheese over and serve.

Mouthwatering Chicken Sandwiches

Time: 17 Minutes
Servings: 4

Ingredients

- Eight chicken slices; cooked and cut into thirds
- A sliced red pepper
- 80g BBQ sauce
- 300g butter lettuce leaves; torn
- A sliced yellow pepper
- Three pita pockets; halved
- Two tablespoon honey
- Two tomatoes; sliced

Directions:

1. Combine the honey with BBQ sauce in a bowl and whisk well.
2. Brush chicken and peppers with some of this combine; transfer to the drawer of your Ninja Dual Zone Air Fryer, select AIR FRY and cook at 175°C, for four mins.
3. Shake the drawer and cook them for an additional two mins. Stuff pita pockets with this cooked lamb mix, tomatoes and lettuce; spread the remaining BBQ sauce and serve.

Chicken Wings

Time: 55 Minutes

Servings: 4

Ingredients

- 1.36kg chicken wings
- 180g potato starch
- 125g butter
- 15g of old bay seasoning
- 5ml lemon juice
- Lemon wedges

Directions:

1. Combine the old bay seasoning with starch and chicken wings in a large bowl and toss well.
2. Transfer the wings to the drawer of your Ninja Dual Zone Air Fryer, insert the drawer into the unit, select AIR FRY at 180°C, and set the time to thirty-five mins. Then press START/STOP to begin.
3. Then rise the temp to 200°C and keep cooking for an additional ten mins. Transfer them to serving plates.
4. Preheat a pan over medium heat with butter to melt it
5. Then pour the lemon juice and stir to combine.
6. Drizzle the butter mixture over the chicken wings and serve with the lemon wedges.
7. Serve them for lunch with lemon wedges on the side.

Special Seafood Stew

Time: 30 Minutes

Servings: 4

Ingredients

- 140g white rice
- 80g sea bass fillet; skinless, boneless, and chopped.
- 60g peas
- 200g mussels
- Six scallops
- 80ml water
- 60g squid pieces
- 80g clams
- Four shrimp
- Four crayfish
- A chopped red pepper
- 400ml vegetable broth
- 15ml olive oil
- Salt and black pepper

Directions:

1. In the drawer of your Ninja Dual Zone Air Fryer; combine sea bass with scallops, shrimp, crayfish, clams, mussels and squid, pour oil over, season with some salt & pepper and toss to coat.
2. Combine peas with red pepper, rice and salt & pepper in a bowl and stir.
3. Add the mixture along with the vegetable broth and water to the seafood in the drawer and insert the drawer into the unit.
4. Select BAKE at 200ºC and set the time to twenty mins. Then press START/STOP to start, stirring halfway. Transfer to serving bowls and serve.

Beef Garlic Pizzas

Time: 20 Minutes

Servings: 4

Ingredients

- Four frozen dinner rolls
- Four minced garlic cloves
- 250g tomato sauce
- Eight cooked and chopped beef slices
- 3g oregano dried
- 3g garlic powder
- 300g grated cheddar cheese
- Cooking spray

Directions:

1. Put the rolls on your working board and press them to get four ovals, spray them using cooking spray and place half in the first drawer and the second half in the second drawer, insert the drawers into the Ninja Dual Zone Air Fryer, set zone 1 to BAKE at 187ºC and set the time to two mins. Select the "MATCH" choice to apply the settings of the first zone to the second zone. Then press START/STOP to start.
2. Next, spread the tomato sauce over each oval, add garlic, garlic powder, and oregano, and top with beef & cheese.
3. Add your pizzas back to the drawers of your Ninja Dual Zone Air Fryer and cook them at 187ºC, for an additional eight mins. Serve them warm.

Tasty Hash Brown Toasts

Time: 17 Minutes

Servings: 4

Ingredients

- Four frozen hash brown patties
- 15ml balsamic vinegar
- 15g chopped basil
- 45g shredded mozzarella
- 30g parmesan; grated
- 15ml olive oil
- 60g chopped cherry tomatoes

Directions:

1. In the first step, arrange the hash brown patties in the drawer of your Ninja Dual Zone Air Fryer and drizzle the oil over them.
2. Select AIR FRY at 200ºC and set the time to seven mins. Then press START/STOP to start.
3. Combine the mozzarella with tomatoes, vinegar, parmesan, and basil in a bowl and stir well. Transfer the hash brown patties to serving plates; add tomatoes combine on top and serve.

Cheese Burgers

Time: 30 Minutes

Servings: 2

Ingredients

- 340g ground lean beef
- 10g mustard
- Four cheddar cheese slices
- 20g ketchup
- Two halved burger buns
- 45g yellow onion; chopped.
- Salt and black pepper

Directions:

1. Combine onion with beef, mustard, ketchup, salt & pepper in a bowl stir well, then shape four patties out of this combination.
2. Add cheese to two patties and cover with the remaining patties.
3. Arrange them in the drawer of your preheated Ninja Dual Zone Air Fryer, Select AIR FRY at 187°C and set the time to twenty mins. Then press START/STOP to start.
4. Add cheeseburger on two bun halves, cover with the other halves and serve.

Japanese Style Chicken

Time: 18 Minutes
Servings: 2

Ingredients

- Two chicken thighs; skinless and boneless
- 30ml sake
- Three minced garlic cloves
- 3ml sesame oil
- 40ml water
- 60ml soy sauce
- 60g mirin
- Two chopped ginger slices
- 30g sugar
- 15g Cornflour mixed with 30ml water
- Sesame seeds (optional)

Directions:

1. Combine chicken thighs with mirin, ginger, soy sauce, sake, garlic, oil, water, sugar, and Cornflour in a bowl toss well, and transfer to the drawer of your preheated Ninja Dual Zone Air Fryer.
2. Select AIR FRY at 180°C and set the time to eight mins. Then press START/STOP to start.
3. Transfer to serving plates, add sesame seeds over and serve.

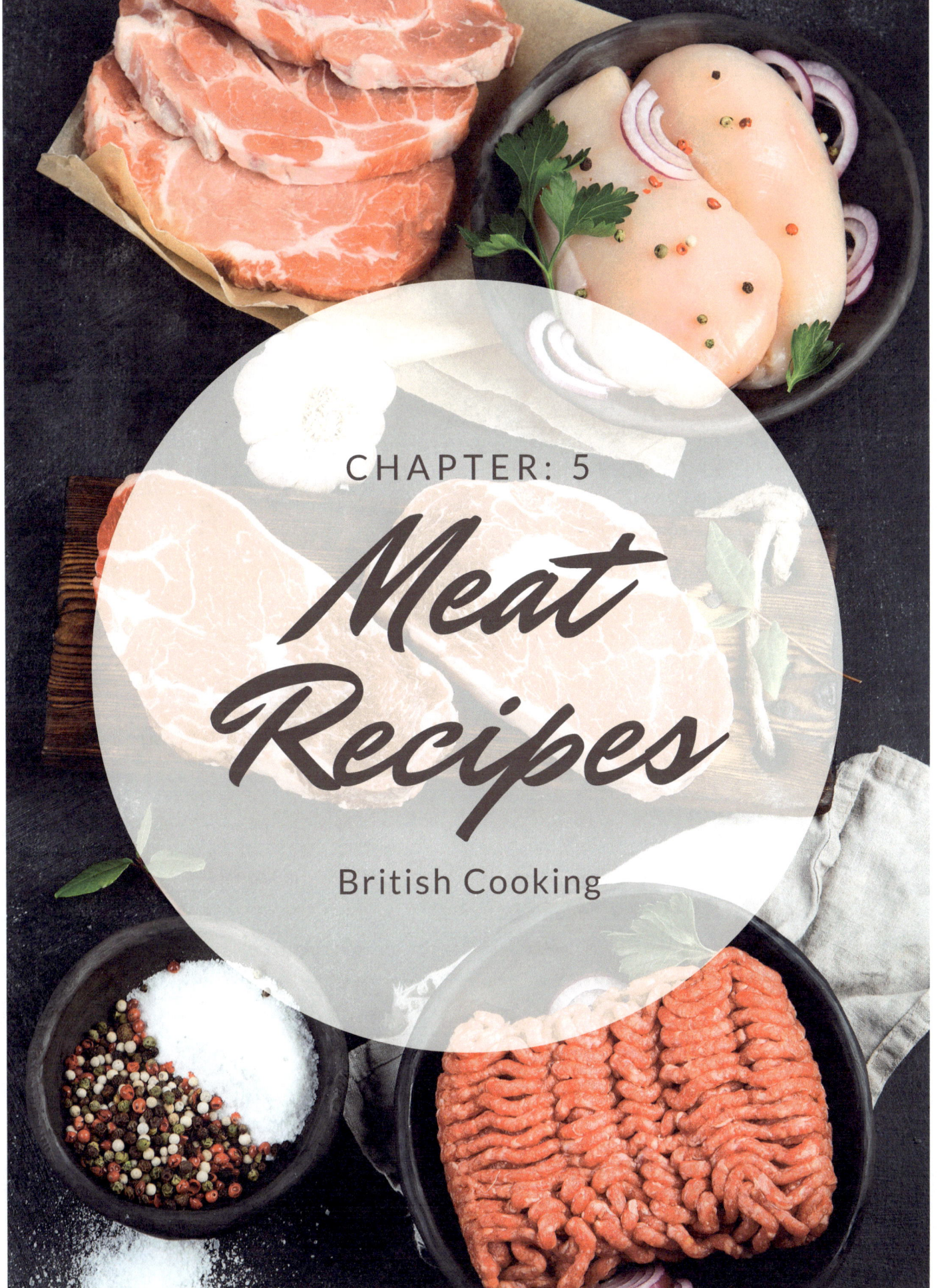

CHAPTER: 5
Meat Recipes
British Cooking

Garlic Lamb Chops Recipe

Time: 20 Minutes

Servings: 4

Ingredients

- Eight lamb chops
- 45ml olive oil
- Four minced garlic cloves
- 15g chopped oregano
- 15g chopped coriander
- Salt and black pepper

Directions:

1. Combine garlic with oregano, salt & pepper, oil, and lamb chops in a bowl and toss to coat.
2. Divide the lamb chops between the drawers of your Ninja Dual Zone Air Fryer,
3. Insert both drawers into the unit, set zone 1 to ROAST at 200°C and set the time to ten mins. Select the "MATCH" choice to apply the settings of the first zone to the second zone. Then press START/STOP to start.
4. Transfer to serving plates and serve.

Beef Brisket and Onion Sauce

Time: 2 h 10 Mins

Servings: 6

Ingredients

- 450g chopped yellow onion
- 225g chopped celery
- Eight earl grey tea bags
- 450g chopped carrot
- 1.8kg beef brisket
- Salt and black pepper
- 1 L water

For the sauce:
- 450g chopped canned tomatoes
- Eight earl grey tea bags
- 450g chopped sweet onion
- 250g Light brown sugar
- 120ml vegetable oil
- 225g chopped celery
- 30g minced garlic
- 250ml white vinegar

Directions:

1. In the first step, pour the water into a heatproof dish that matches the drawer of your Ninja Dual Zone Air Fryer, add carrot, yellow onion, 225g celery, salt & pepper; stir and bring to a simmer over medium-high heat. Next, add beef brisket and the tea bags; stir.
2. Place the dish in the drawer of your Ninja Dual Zone Air Fryer and insert it into the unit, Select ROAST at 150ºC and set the time to an hour and thirty mins. Then press START/STOP to start.
3. Meantime, preheat a pan with the vegetable oil over medium-high heat, add the sweet onion; stir and sauté for ten mins. Then add all the remaining sauce ingredients and stir, bring to a simmer, cook for ten mins and remove tea bags from the sauce.
4. Place the cooked beef on your cutting board, slice, transfer to serving plates, drizzle the sauce over and serve.

Beef Patties & Mushroom Sauce

Time: 35 Minutes

Servings: 6

Ingredients

- 500g ground beef
- 3g garlic powder
- 60ml beef stock
- 180g flour
- 15g chopped parsley
- 15g onion flakes
- 15ml soy sauce
- Salt and black pepper

For the sauce:
- 250g chopped yellow onion
- 3ml soy sauce
- 60g sour cream
- 125ml beef stock
- 500g sliced mushrooms
- 30g beef Fat
- 30g butter
- Salt and black pepper

Directions:

1. Combine the ground beef with garlic powder, salt & pepper, 60ml beef stock, flour, 15ml soy sauce, parsley, and onion flakes; stir well, shape six patties out of this mixture, arrange them in the drawer of your Ninja Dual Zone Air Fryer and insert the drawer into the unit.
2. Select AIR FRY at 175°C and set the time to fourteen mins. Then press START/STOP to start
3. Meantime; preheat a pan with the beef fat and butter over medium heat, add the sliced mushrooms; stir and cook for four mins, then add onions; stir and cook for an additional four mins.
4. Add all the remaining ingredients bring to a simmer and take off the heat.
5. Transfer the beef patties to serving plates and serve the sauce.

Beef Stuffed Squash Recipe

Time: 50 Minutes

Servings: 2

Ingredients

- 450g ground beef
- A pricked spaghetti squash
- 1g cayenne pepper
- 3g dried thyme
- 800g chopped canned tomatoes
- 5g dried oregano
- Salt and black pepper
- Three minced garlic cloves
- A chopped yellow onion
- A sliced Portobello mushroom
- A chopped green pepper

Directions:

1. Place the spaghetti squash in the drawer of your Ninja Dual Zone Air Fryer, select BAKE at 175ºC and set the time to twenty mins. Then press START/STOP to start.
2. Then place it on a cutting board, cut it into halves and remove the seeds.
3. Preheat a pan over medium-high heat, add onion, meat and mushroom, and garlic; stir and cook until the meat becomes brown.
4. Add salt & pepper with all the remaining; stir and cook for an additional ten mins.
5. Stuff squash with this meat combine and place it in the drawer of your Ninja Dual Zone Air Fryer. Select AIR FRY at 180ºC and set the time to ten mins. Then press START/STOP to start. Transfer to serving plates and serve.

Beef & Green Onions Marinade

Time: 30 Minutes

Servings: 4

Ingredients

- 250g chopped green onion
- Five minced garlic cloves
- 60g Light brown sugar
- 250ml soy sauce
- 125ml water
- 5g black pepper
- 60g sesame seeds
- 450g lean beef

Directions:

1. Combine onion with sugar, sesame seeds, soy sauce, water, garlic and black pepper in a bowl, whisk, add meat, toss and leave aside for ten mins.
2. Drain beef, transfer to the drawer of your preheated Ninja dual zone air fryer, Select ROAST and cook at 200ºC, for twenty mins. Slice, transfer to serving plates, and serve.

Beef Curry Recipe

Time: 55 Minutes

Servings: 4

Ingredients

- 900g beef steak; cubed
- 280ml canned coconut milk
- Two chopped yellow onions
- Two minced garlic cloves
- 15ml mustard
- 35g curry powder
- 30ml tomato sauce
- 30ml olive oil
- Three cubed potatoes
- Salt and black pepper

Directions:

1. Preheat a pan that matches the drawer of your Ninja dual zone air fryer with the oil over medium-high heat, add garlic and onions; stir and cook for four mins, then add mustard along with potatoes; stir and cook for one min.
2. Add the meat with the curry powder, salt & pepper, coconut milk, and tomato sauce; stir, transfer to the drawer, insert the drawer into the unit, Select ROAST and cook at 180ºC, for forty mins. transfer to serving bowls and serve.

Sirloin Steaks & Pico De Gallo

Time: 20 Minutes
Servings: 4

Ingredients

- 30g chilli powder
- Four medium sirloin steaks
- 5g onion powder
- 5g garlic powder
- 5g cumin; ground
- 7g sweet paprika
- Salt and black pepper

For the Pico de gallo:

- A chopped small red onion
- Two minced garlic cloves
- A chopped small green pepper
- A chopped jalapeno
- Two chopped tomatoes
- 30ml lime juice
- 60g chopped Coriander
- 1g ground cumin

Directions:

1. Combine the chilli powder with a pinch of salt, black pepper, onion powder, garlic powder, paprika, and one tsp of cumin in a bowl; stir well, use this mixture to season steaks, and place them in the drawer of your preheated Ninja dual zone air fryer. Select ROAST and cook at 180°C, for ten mins.
2. Combine tomatoes with the red onion, garlic, lime juice, Coriander, pepper, jalapeno, black pepper to the taste, and 1/4 tsp of cumin and toss.
3. Transfer the steaks to serving plates, add the mixture over and serve immediately.

Balsamic Beef Recipe

Time: 1 h 10 Mins

Servings: 6

Ingredients

- 125ml balsamic vinegar
- 15ml Worcestershire sauce
- 15g honey
- 15ml soy sauce
- 250ml beef stock
- A medium beef roast
- Four minced garlic cloves

Directions:

1. Combine the beef roast with Worcestershire sauce, vinegar, stock, honey, soy sauce, and garlic in a heatproof dish that matches the drawer of your preheated Ninja dual zone air fryer, toss well and place it in the drawer. Select ROAST and cook at 187°C, for 60 mins.
2. Slice the cooked meat, transfer to serving plates, drizzle the sauce on top and serve.

Beef Casserole Recipe

Time: 65 Minutes

Servings: 12

Ingredients

- 800g chopped canned tomatoes
- 15ml olive oil
- 500g ground beef
- 500g chopped Aubergine
- 10g gluten-free Worcestershire sauce
- 500g grated mozzarella
- 450ml tomato sauce
- 10g mustard
- 30g chopped parsley
- 5g dried oregano
- Salt and black pepper

Directions:

1. Combine Aubergine with salt & pepper and oil in a bowl and toss to coat.
2. In a separate bowl, combine the beef with mustard, Worcestershire sauce, salt & pepper stir well and transfer to the bottom of a pan that matches the drawer of your preheated Ninja dual zone air fryer.
3. Add the mixture you've made in the first step with the tomato sauce, tomatoes, parsley, and oregano and sprinkle mozzarella on top.
4. Place the pan into the drawer and insert it inside the unit, Select ROAST and cook at 180ºC, for thirty-five mins. Transfer to serving plates, and serve immediately!

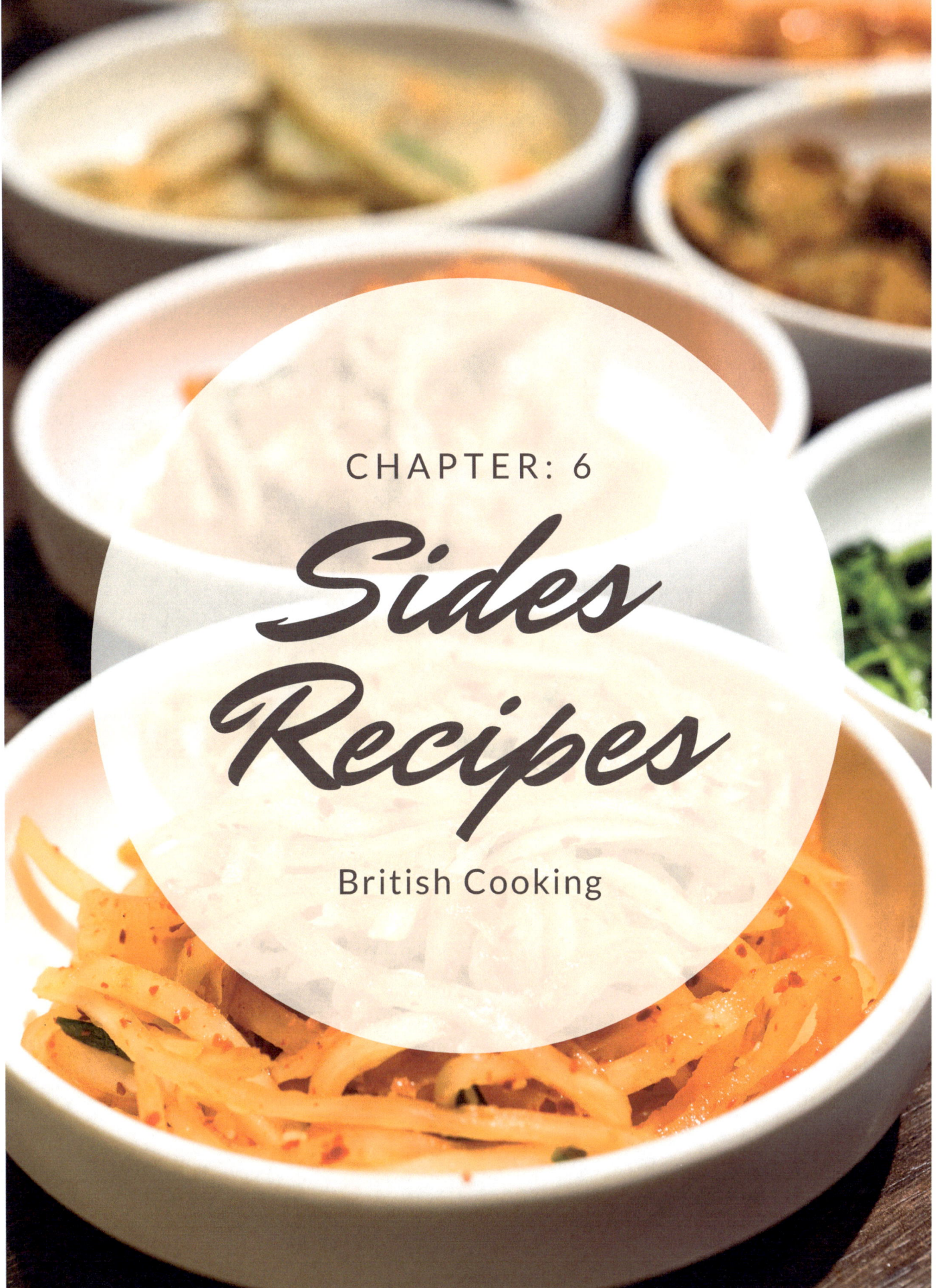

CHAPTER: 6
Sides Recipes
British Cooking

Fried Creamy Cabbage

Time: 30 Minutes

Servings: 4

Ingredients

- A chopped green cabbage head
- 250g whipped cream
- A chopped yellow onion
- Four chopped lamb slices
- 30g Cornflour
- Salt and black pepper

Directions:

1. Place the lamb slices, cabbage and onion in the drawer of your Ninja dual zone air fryer.
2. Combine the cream with Cornflour, salt & pepper, stir, and add the mixture over the cabbage mix. Toss.
3. Insert the drawer into the unit, select AIR FRY and cook at 200°C, for twenty mins; transfer to serving plates and serve.

Brussels Sprouts Dish

Time: 25 Minutes

Servings: 4

Ingredients

- 450g trimmed and halved Brussels sprouts
- 30ml olive oil
- 3g chopped thyme
- 125g mayonnaise
- 30g crushed roasted garlic
- Salt and black pepper

Directions:

1. Combine Brussels sprouts with salt & pepper and oil in the drawer of your Ninja dual zone air fryer; toss well and insert the drawer into the unit.
2. Select AIR FRY at 200ºC and set the time to fifteen mins, Press START/STOP to begin cooking.
3. Meantime, combine mayo with thyme and garlic and whisk well. Transfer the sprouts serving plate; drizzle garlic sauce on top and serve.

Brussels Sprouts & Pomegranate

Time: 15 Minutes

Servings: 4

Ingredients

- 450g trimmed and halved Brussels sprouts
- 60g toasted pine nuts
- 15ml olive oil
- 30ml veggie stock
- 250g pomegranate seeds
- Salt & black pepper

Directions:

1. Combine the Brussels sprouts with salt, pepper, and all the other ingredients in a heat-proof dish that matches the drawer of your Ninja dual zone air fryer stir, and place the dish in the drawer.
2. Insert the drawer into the unit, select AIR FRY at 200°C and set the time to ten mins, Press START/STOP to begin cooking.
3. Transfer to serving plates and serve.

Onion Rings Dish

Time: 20 Minutes

Servings: 3

Ingredients

- An onion cut into medium slices and rings separated
- An egg
- 250ml milk
- 180g bread crumbs
- 300g white flour
- 5g baking powder
- A pinch of salt

Directions:

1. Combine the flour with salt and baking powder in a bowl; stir, dredge onion rings in this combination and place them on a plate
2. Now pour milk and add egg to the flour combination and whisk well
3. Dip onion rings in this combination and dredge them in breadcrumbs.
4. Place the rings in the drawer of your Ninja dual zone air fryer, select AIR FRY and cook them at 180ºC, for ten mins.
5. Transfer to serving plates and serve.

Mushrooms and Cream

Time: 20 Minutes
Servings: 6

Ingredients

- Two chopped beef bacon strips
- A chopped yellow onion
- 125g sour cream
- 250g grated cheddar cheese
- A chopped green pepper
- Twentyfour mushrooms; stems removed
- A grated carrot
- Salt and black pepper

Directions:

1. Preheat a pan over medium high heat; add beef, onion, green pepper and carrot; stir and cook for one min.
2. Add sour cream along with salt & pepper, stir cook for an additional min; take off the heat and cool down.
3. Stuff mushrooms with this combine, sprinkle cheese over and place half in the first drawer and the second half in the second drawer, insert the drawers into the Ninja Dual Zone Air Fryer, set zone 1 to AIR FRY at 180ºC and set the time to eight mins. Select the "MATCH" choice to apply the settings of the first zone to the second zone. Then press START/STOP to start. Transfer to serving plates and serve!

Roasted Peppers Dish

Time: 30 Minutes

Servings: 4

Ingredients

- Four red peppers; cut into medium strips
- Four yellow peppers; cut into medium strips
- Four green peppers; cut into medium strips
- A chopped yellow onion
- 15g sweet paprika
- 15ml olive oil
- Salt and black pepper

Directions:

1. Combine all the peppers in the drawer of your Ninja Dual Zone Air Fryer.
2. Add the remaining mentioned ingredients; toss and insert the drawer into the unit.
3. Select ROAST at 175°C and set the time to twenty mins, then press START/STOP to start. Divide among plates and serve!

Delicious Cauliflower Cakes

Time: 20 Minutes

Servings: 6

Ingredients

- Two eggs
- 125g grated parmesan
- 60g white flour
- 800g cauliflower rice
- Salt and black pepper
- Cooking spray

Directions:

1. Combine cauliflower rice with salt & pepper in a bowl, stir and squeeze excess water.
2. Now place the cauliflower and place it in a separate bowl; add eggs, salt & pepper, flour and parmesan; stir well and shape cakes out of the mixture
3. Grease the drawer of your Ninja Dual Zone Air Fryer with cooking spray and preheat it to 200 C; arrange the cakes into the drawer and cook them for ten mins on the AIR FRY mode flipping them halfway. Transfer to serving plates and serve.

Beet Fries Dish

Time: 25 Minutes

Servings: 4

Ingredients

- Four Beetroot; washed, peeled, and cut into fries
- Two minced garlic cloves
- 5ml lemon juice
- 15ml olive oil
- Salt and black

Directions:

1. Combine Beetroot with oil, salt, pepper, garlic, and lemon juice in a bowl; toss well, and transfer them to the drawer of your Ninja Dual Zone Air Fryer.
2. Select AIR FRY at 200°C and set the time to fifteen mins.
3. Transfer to serving plates and serve.

Pumpkin Rice Dish

Time: 35 Minutes

Servings: 4

Ingredients

- 340g white rice
- 5g chopped thyme
- 3g nutmeg
- 3g allspice
- 3g grated ginger
- 3g cinnamon powder
- 1 L chicken stock
- 170g pumpkin puree
- 30ml olive oil
- A chopped small yellow onion
- Two minced garlic cloves
- 110g Double cream

Directions:

1. Combine oil with onion, garlic, rice, stock, pumpkin puree, nutmeg, thyme, ginger, cinnamon, allspice and cream in a dish that matches the drawer of your Ninja Dual Zone Air Fryer.
2. Place the dish in the drawer and insert the drawer into the unit, select ROAST at 180°C, for thirty mins. Divide among plates and serve!

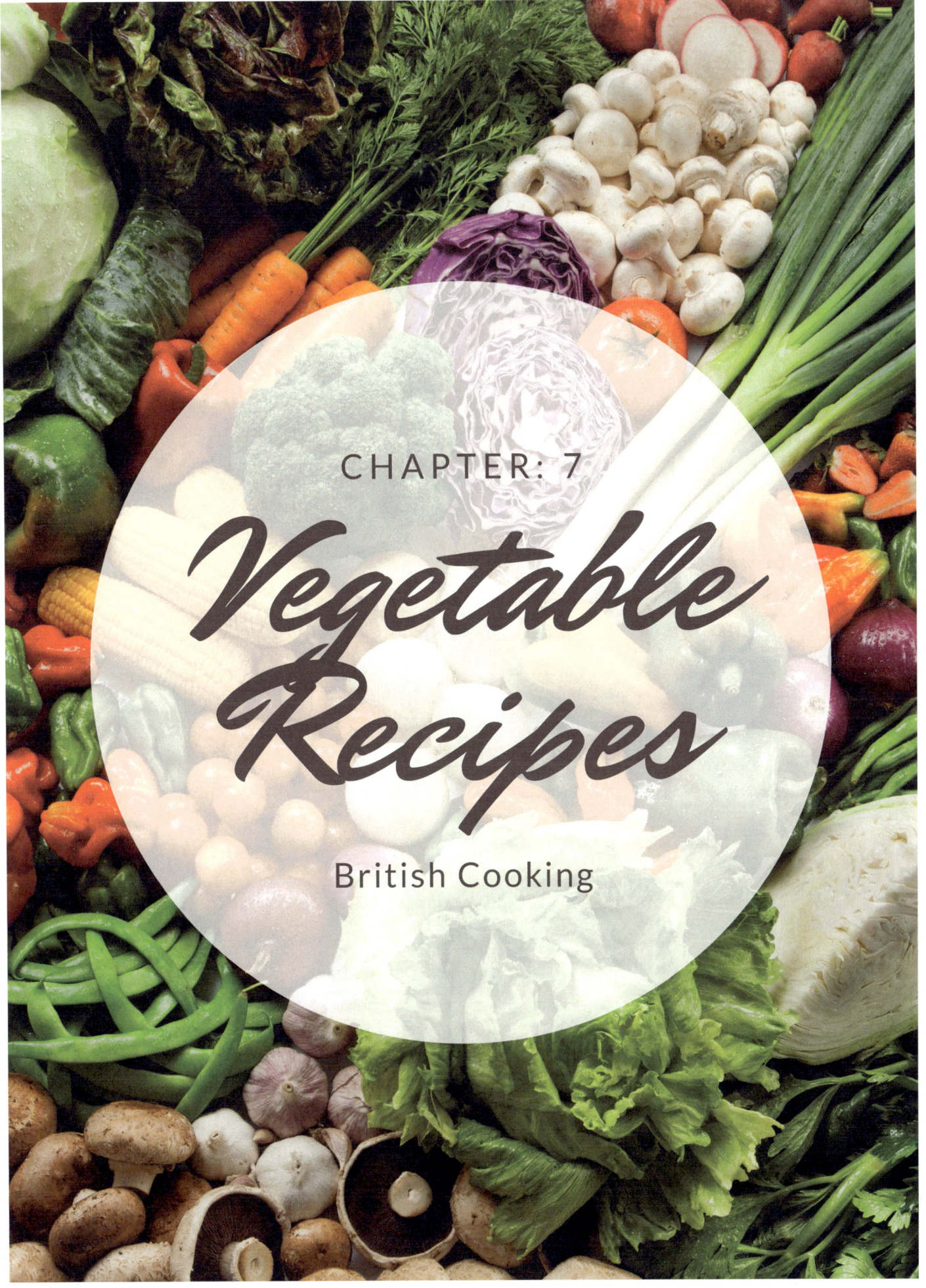

CHAPTER: 7

Vegetable Recipes

British Cooking

Simple Tomatoes & Red Pepper Sauce

Time: 25 Minutes

Servings: 4

Ingredients

- Two chopped red peppers
- 3 bay leaves
- 2 garlic cloves; minced
- 450g cherry tomatoes; halved
- 5g rosemary; dried
- 30ml olive oil
- 15ml balsamic vinegar
- Salt and black pepper to the taste

Directions:

1. Combine the tomatoes with garlic, salt & black pepper, rosemary, bay leaves, 1/2 of the oil and 1/2 of the vinegar in a bowl, toss to coat, and transfer to the drawer of your Ninja Dual Zone Air Fryer.
2. Insert the drawer into the unit, and select ROAST at 160ºC, for fifteen mins.
3. Meantime; combine the red peppers with a pinch of sea salt, black pepper, the remaining oil and the remaining vinegar in your food processor and blend everything well together.
4. Transfer the cooked tomatoes to serving plates, drizzle the red pepper sauce on top and serve.

Mexican Peppers Recipe

Time: 35 Minutes

Servings: 4

Ingredients

- Four chicken breasts
- Four red peppers; tops cut off and seeds removed
- 250g chopped tomatoes
- 30g chopped jarred jalapenos
- 3g crushed red pepper
- 125ml tomato juice
- 60g chopped yellow onion
- 60g chopped green peppers
- 500g tomato sauce
- 3g garlic powder
- 5g chilli powder
- Salt and black pepper
- 10g onion powder
- 5g cumin; ground

Directions:

1. Combine the chicken breasts with tomato juice, jalapenos, tomatoes, onion, green peppers, salt, pepper, onion powder, red pepper, chilli powder, garlic powder, oregano, and cumin in a pan that matches the drawer of your Ninja Dual Zone Air Fryer; stir well.
2. Transfer the pan to the drawer of your Ninja Dual Zone Air Fryer, insert the drawer into the unit, and select AIR FRY at 175ºC, for fifteen mins.
3. Next, shred meat using two forks; stir, stuff the red peppers with this combination, add them to the drawer of your machine, select ROAST and cook at 160ºC, for an additional ten mins. Enjoy!

Asian Potatoes Recipe

Time: 22 Minutes

Servings: 4

Ingredients

- 15g coriander seeds
- 15g chopped pickled mango
- 15g cumin seeds
- 10g fenugreek; dried
- 3g turmeric powder
- 3g red chilli powder
- 5g pomegranate powder
- Five potatoes; boiled, peeled and cubed
- Salt and black pepper
- 30ml olive oil

Directions:

1. Preheat a pan that matches the drawer of your Ninja Dual Zone Air Fryer with the oil over medium heat, add coriander and cumin seeds; stir and cook for two mins.
2. Add all the remaining ingredients, toss, place the pan in the drawer of your Ninja Dual Zone Air Fryer, and insert the drawer into the unit.
3. Select ROAST at 180ºC, for ten mins. Enjoy!

Green Beans and Parmesan

Time: 18 Minutes

Servings: 4

Ingredients

- 340g green beans
- A whisked egg
- 80g grated parmesan
- 10g minced garlic
- 30ml olive oil
- Salt and black pepper

Directions:

1. Combine the oil with salt, pepper, garlic and egg in a bowl and whisk well.
2. Add green beans to this mix, toss well and sprinkle parmesan all over.
3. Transfer green beans to the drawer of your Ninja Dual Zone Air Fryer, select AIR FRY and cook them at 200ºC, for eight. Divide them between plates and serve them immediately.

Broccoli Hash Recipe

Time: 38 Minutes

Servings: 2

Ingredients

- 280g mushrooms; halved
- 5g basil; dried
- 15ml balsamic vinegar
- A peeled and pitted avocado
- A broccoli head; florets separated
- A chopped yellow onion
- 15ml olive oil
- A minced garlic clove
- A pinch of red pepper flakes
- Salt and black pepper

Directions:

1. Combine the mushrooms with broccoli, onion, garlic and avocado in a bowl.
2. Combine vinegar, oil, salt, pepper and basil in a separate bowl and whisk well and add this mixture over the veggies, toss to coat, and leave it aside for thirty mins.
3. Transfer to the drawer of your Ninja Dual Zone Air Fryer, select ROAST and cook at 175ºC, for eight mins.
4. Divide them between plates and serve with pepper flakes on top.

Broccoli Salad Recipe

Time: 18 Minutes

Servings: 4

Ingredients

- A broccoli head; florets separated
- Six minced garlic cloves
- 15ml peanut oil
- 15ml apple cider vinegar
- Salt and black pepper

Directions:

1. Combine the broccoli with salt & pepper, and 1/2 of the oil in a bowl, toss, transfer to the drawer of your Ninja Dual Zone Air Fryer, select ROAST and cook at 175°C, for eight mins; shaking the drawer halfway.
2. Place the cooked broccoli in a salad bowl, add garlic, the remaining oil and apple cider vinegar, toss and serve.

Peppers Stuffed with Beef

Time: 65 Minutes

Servings: 4

Ingredients

- 450g ground beef
- Four red peppers; cut into halves and seeds removed
- 80g chopped walnuts
- 80g raisins
- 15g hot curry powder
- An egg
- 30ml olive oil
- 15g ginger; grated
- 5g coriander; ground
- A chopped onion
- Three minced garlic cloves
- 3g turmeric powder
- 3g cumin; ground
- Salt and black pepper

Directions:

1. Preheat a pan with the oil over medium-high heat, add onion; stir and cook for four mins, then add garlic and beef; stir and cook for ten mins.
2. Add the remaining mentioned ingredients except for the peppers and egg; stir and take off the heat and then mix with the egg.
3. Next, stuff pepper halves with this mixture, and arrange them in the drawer of your Ninja Dual Zone Air Fryer.
4. Select AIR FRY and cook at 160ºC, for twenty min. Transfer to serving plates and serve.

Potatoes and Special Tomato Sauce

Time: 26 Minutes

Servings: 4

Ingredients

- 900g potatoes; cubed
- 30g basil; chopped.
- Four minced garlic cloves
- A chopped yellow onion
- 3g dried oregano
- 3g dried parsley
- 250g tomato sauce
- 30ml olive oil

Directions:

1. Preheat a pan that matches the drawer of your Ninja Dual Zone Air Fryer with the oil over medium heat, add onion; stir and cook for one to two mins.
2. Add the remaining mentioned ingredients except for basil, transfer to the drawer of your Ninja Dual Zone Air Fryer, select ROAST and cook at 187°C, for sixteen mins.
3. Add basil, toss, transfer to serving plates and serve.

Stuffed Poblano Peppers

Time: 25 Minutes

Servings: 4

Ingredients

- Ten poblano peppers
- 125g chopped coriander
- A chopped white onion
- 15ml olive oil
- 10g minced garlic
- 225g chopped mushrooms
- Salt and black pepper

Directions:

1. Preheat a pan with the oil over medium-high heat, add mushrooms & onion; stir and cook for five mins, then add coriander, garlic, salt & black pepper; stir and cook for an additional two mins.
2. Fill the poblanos with this mixture, arrange them into the drawer of your Ninja Dual Zone Air Fryer, select AIR FRY and cook at 175°C, for fifteen mins. Enjoy!

CHAPTER: 8

Starters Recipes

British Cooking

Herbed Tomatoes

Time: 30 Minutes

Servings: 2

Ingredients

- Two halved tomatoes
- 5g dried oregano
- 5g dried parsley
- 5g dried basil
- 5g dried rosemary
- Cooking spray
- Salt and black pepper

Directions:

1. Use the cooking oil to spray tomato halves, and season with salt & pepper, oregano, parsley, basil, and then rosemary on top.
2. Transfer to the drawer of your Ninja Dual Zone Air Fryer, select ROAST and cook at 160°C, for twenty mins.
3. Place them on a serving plate and serve.

Chestnut and Shrimp Rolls

Time: 25 Minutes

Servings: 4

Ingredients

- 225g chopped, already cooked shrimp
- 225g chopped water chestnuts
- 30ml olive oil
- A minced garlic clove
- 5g grated ginger
- Three chopped spring onions
- 15ml water
- An egg yolk
- 225g chopped shiitake mushrooms
- 500g chopped cabbage
- Six spring roll wrappers
- Salt and black pepper

Directions:

1. Preheat a pan with the oil over medium-high heat, add shrimp, mushrooms, chestnuts, cabbage, spring onions, garlic, ginger, salt & pepper; stir and cook for two mins.
2. Combine the egg with water in a small bowl and stir whisk. Arrange roll wrappers on your working board, divide the mixture you've made in the first step on them, and seal edges with egg wash.
3. Divide them between the drawers of your Ninja Dual Zone Air Fryer, and insert both drawers into the unit.
4. Set zone 1 to AIR FRY at 180ºC and set the time to fifteen mins. Select the "MATCH" choice to apply the settings of the first zone to the second zone. Then press START/STOP to start. Transfer to serving plates and serve.

Tasty Crab Sticks

Time: 30 Minutes

Servings: 4

Ingredients

- Ten halved crabsticks
- 10g Cajun seasoning
- 10ml sesame oil

Directions:

1. In a bowl; combine the crab sticks with Cajun seasoning and sesame oil; toss.
2. Divide the sticks between the drawers of your Ninja Dual Zone Air Fryer, and insert both drawers into the unit.
3. Set zone 1 to AIR FRY at 175ºC and set the time to twelve mins. Select the "MATCH" choice to apply the settings of the first zone to the second zone. Then press START/STOP to start. Transfer to serving plates and serve.

Tasty Fish Sticks

Time: 22 Minutes

Servings: 2

Ingredients

- Four white fish filets; boneless, skinless, and cut into medium sticks
- 60ml olive oil
- A whisked egg
- 120g bread crumbs
- Salt and black pepper

Directions:

1. Combine bread crumbs with oil in a bowl and stir well, and whisk the egg with salt & pepper in a separate bowl.
2. Dip your sticks in the egg mix and then in bread crumbs. place them in the drawer of your Ninja Dual Zone Air Fryer, select AIR FRY and cook at 180°C, for twelve mins.
3. Transfer to a serving plate and serve.

Mouthwatering Beef Rolls

Time: 24 Minutes

Servings: 4

Ingredients

- 900g beef steak; opened and flattened with a meat tenderizer
- 90g roasted and chopped red pepper
- 250g baby spinach
- 45g pesto
- Six slices of provolone cheese
- Salt and black pepper

Directions:

1. Place the beef steak on your cutting surface, spread pesto over it, add cheese in a single layer, and add spinach, red peppers, and salt & pepper to the taste, then roll your steak, seal it using toothpicks, and add more salt and pepper to season.
2. Transfer it to the drawer of your Ninja Dual Zone Air Fryer, select AIR FRY and cook at 200ºC, for fifteen mins; rotating it halfway.
3. When it's completed, let the roll cool down, cut into 6cm rolls, and transfer to a serving plate and serve.

Delicious Shrimp Muffins

Time: 36 Minutes

Servings: 6

Ingredients

- A peeled and halved spaghetti squash
- 30g mayonnaise
- 380g panko
- 5g parsley flakes
- 250g mozzarella; shredded.
- 220g peeled, cooked, and chopped shrimp
- A minced garlic clove
- Salt and black pepper
- Cooking spray

Directions:

1. Place squash halves in the drawer of your Ninja Dual Zone Air Fryer; select ROAST and cook at 175°C, for sixteen mins; let it cool down and scrape flesh into a bowl.
2. Add shrimp, parsley flakes, salt & pepper, panko, mozzarella and mayo and stir well.
3. Use the cooking spray to spray a muffin tray that matches the drawer of your Ninja Dual Zone Air Fryer and divide squash and shrimp combine in each cup.
4. Place the tray into the drawer, insert the drawer in the unit, select AIR FRY and cook at 180°C, for ten mins.
5. Transfer to serving plates and serve

Quick Courgette Cakes

Time: 22 Minutes

Servings: 12

Ingredients

- 125g whole wheat flour
- 125g chopped dill
- A chopped yellow onion
- Three grated Courgettes
- One egg
- Two minced garlic cloves
- Cooking spray
- Salt and black pepper

Directions:

1. Combine onion with courgettes, flour, garlic, salt & pepper, egg and dill in a bowl; stir well, and shape small patties out of this combination.
2. Use the cooking spray to spray them, divide them between the drawers of your Ninja Dual Zone Air Fryer, and insert both drawers into the unit.
3. Set zone 1 to AIR FRY at 187°C and set the time to six mins. Select the "MATCH" choice to apply the settings of the first zone to the second zone. Then press START/STOP to start. Transfer to serving plates and serve. Serve them immediately.

Tasty Stuffed Peppers

Time: 18 Minutes

Servings: 8

Ingredients

- Eight small red peppers; tops cut off and seeds removed
- 15ml olive oil
- 80g goat cheese; cut into eight pieces
- Salt and black pepper

Directions:

1. Combine cheese with oil with salt & pepper and toss to coat. Stuff the peppers with this cheese, divide them between the drawers of your Ninja Dual Zone Air Fryer, and insert both drawers into the unit. (you can cook them in one zone depending on the size of the peppers)
2. Set zone 1 to AIR FRY at 200°C and set the time to eight mins. Select the "MATCH" choice to apply the settings of the first zone to the second zone. Then press START/STOP to start.
3. Transfer to serving plates and serve.

Tasty Apple Chips

Time: 20 Minutes

Servings: 2

Ingredients

- A cored and sliced apple
- 3g cinnamon powder
- 15g white sugar
- A pinch of salt

Directions:

1. Combine the apple slices with cinnamon and salt & sugar; toss, transfer to that matches the drawer of your Ninja Dual Zone Air Fryer, select DEHYDRATE and cook for ten at 200ºC, flipping once.
2. Transfer to serving bowls and serve.

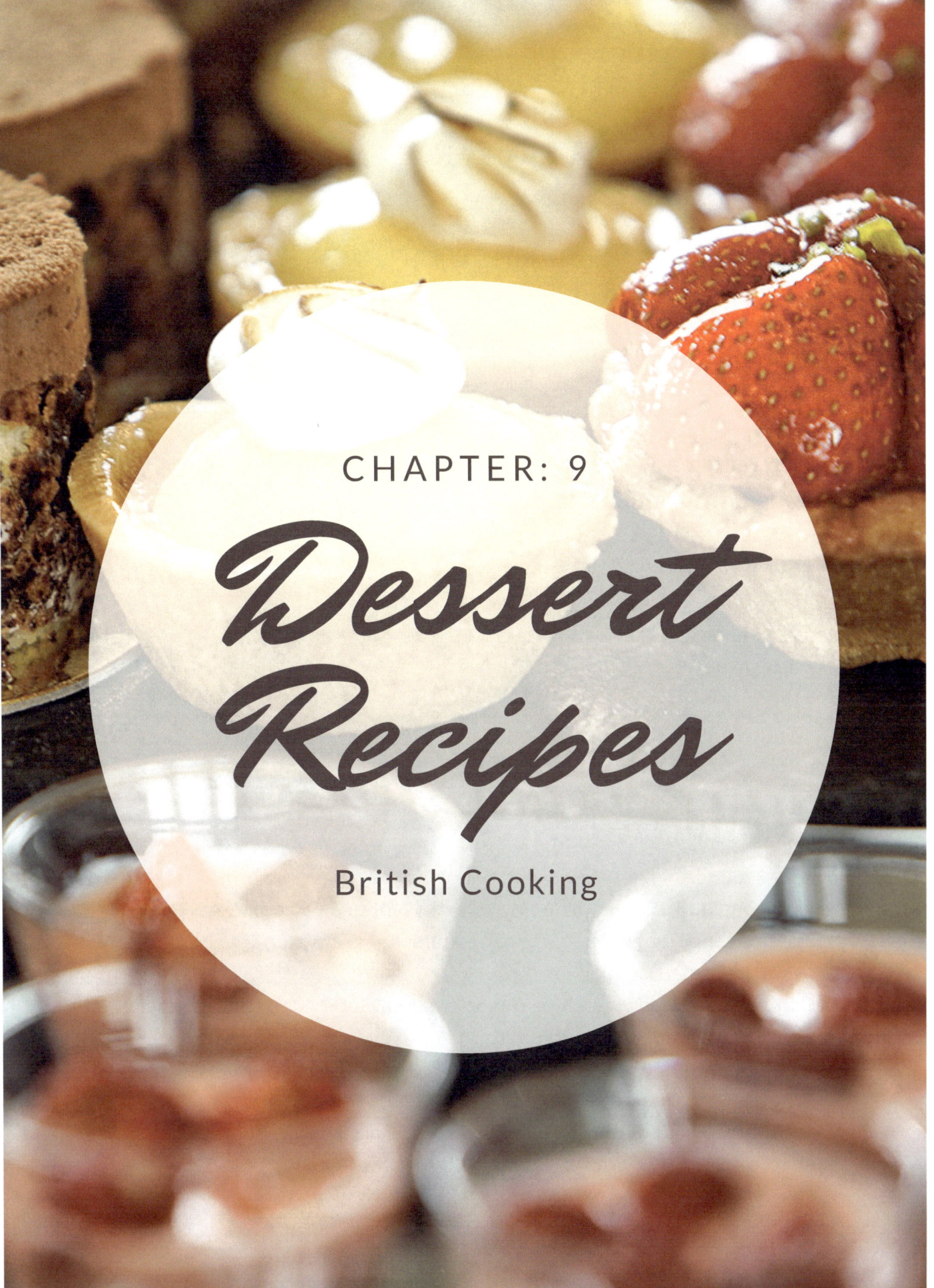

Pumpkin Pie Recipe

Time: 25 Minutes

Servings: 9

Ingredients

- 15g sugar
- 30g flour
- 30ml water
- 15g butter

For the pumpkin pie filling:

- 90g chopped pumpkin flesh
- 80ml water
- 5g nutmeg
- A whisked egg
- 5g mixed spice
- 15g sugar

Directions:

1. Pour 3-ounce of water into a pot, bring to a boil over medium-high heat, add the pumpkin, egg, a tbsp of sugar, nutmeg and spice; stir, boil for twenty mins; take off the heat and blend using an immersion blender
2. Combine the flour with butter, a tbsp of sugar and two tbsp of water and knead your dough well.
3. Grease a pie pan that matches the drawer of your Ninja Dual Zone Air Fryer with butter, place the dough into the pan and press in the bottom and fill with pumpkin pie filling.
4. Put the pane in the drawer and insert the drawer into the unit, Select BAKE and cook at 180ºC, for fifteen mins. Enjoy!

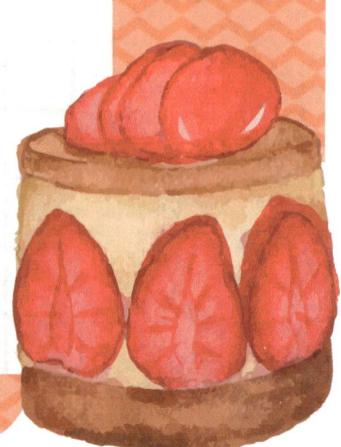

Black Tea Cake

Time: 45 Minutes

Servings: 12

Ingredients

- 90g black tea powder
- 125g butter
- 125ml olive oil
- 850g flour
- 5g Bicarbonate of soda
- 500ml milk
- 500g sugar
- 4 eggs
- 10g vanilla extract
- 15g baking powder

For the cream:

- 90g honey
- 250g soft butter
- 1kg sugar

Directions:

1. Preheat the milk in a pot over medium heat, then add tea and stir well, take off the heat and let it cool down.
2. Combine the milk mix with 125g butter, 500g sugar, eggs, vanilla extract, vegetable oil, 850g flour, baking powder, and Bicarbonate of soda in a large bowl and stir everything really well. Transfer this to two round pans after greasing them.
3. Place the pans in the drawers of your Ninja Dual Zone Air Fryer and insert both drawers into the unit. Set zone 1 to BAKE at 165ºC and set the time to twenty-five mins. Select the "MATCH" choice to apply the settings of the first zone to the second zone. Then press START/STOP to start.
4. Mix all the cream ingredients together in a bowl and stir really well.
5. Transfer one cake to a plate and spread the cream on top of it, add the remaining cake over and keep it in the fridge. Serve it cold!

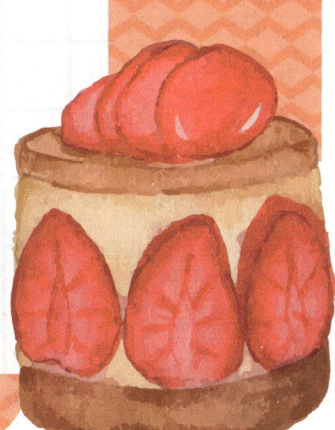

Mini Lava Cakes Recipe

Time: 30 Minutes

Servings: 3

Ingredients

- An egg
- 3g baking powder
- 60g sugar
- 60ml milk
- 30ml olive oil
- 60g flour
- 15g cocoa powder
- 3g orange zest

Directions:

1. Combine sugar with the egg, oil, milk, flour, salt, baking powder, cocoa powder, and orange zest in a bowl; stir very well and transfer the mixture to greased ramekins.
2. Place the ramekins in the drawers of your Ninja Dual Zone Air Fryer and insert both drawers into the unit. Set zone 1 to BAKE at 160ºC and set the time to twenty mins. Select the "MATCH" choice to apply the settings of the first zone to the second zone. Then press START/STOP to start. Serve your cakes warm!

Special Brownies Recipe

Time: 27 Minutes

Servings: 4

Ingredients

- 80g cocoa powder
- 100g butter
- An egg
- 60g chopped walnuts
- 60g white flour
- 3g baking powder
- 3ml vanilla extract
- 80g sugar
- 15g peanut butter

Directions:

1. Preheat a pan with sugar and six tbsp of butter over medium heat; stir, cook for five mins; then place it in a bowl, add salt, cocoa powder, baking powder, vanilla extract, walnuts, egg and flour; stir everything together well and pour into a pan that matches the drawer of your Ninja dual zone air fryer.
2. Combine the peanut butter with a tbsp of butter in a bowl, heat up in your microwave for a bit; stir well and pour it over the mixture in the pan.
3. Place the pan in the drawer of your Ninja dual zone air fryer, select BAKE at 160ºC and bake for seventeen mins.
4. Let it cool down, slice and serve.

Lentils and Dates Brownies

Time: 25 Minutes

Servings: 8

Ingredients

- 800g rinsed and drained canned lentils
- Twelve dates
- 60g almond butter
- A peeled and chopped banana
- 15g honey
- 3g Bicarbonate of soda
- 30g cocoa powder

Directions:

1. Combine butter with banana, lentils, cocoa, Bicarbonate of soda, and honey in your food processor and blend well, then add dates, pulse again more times and pour it into a greased pan that matches the drawer of your Ninja dual zone air fryer.
2. Place the pan in the drawer of your Ninja dual zone air fryer, select BAKE at 180ºC and bake for fifteen mins.
3. When it's completed, leave it to cool down, cut and serve.

Cocoa Cake Recipe

Time: 27 Minutes

Servings: 6

Ingredients

- 90g melted butter
- 80g flour
- Three eggs
- 80g sugar
- 5g cocoa powder
- 3ml lemon juice

Directions:

1. Combine the cocoa powder with a tbsp of butter in a bowl and whisk.
2. Combine the remaining butter with eggs, flour, sugar and lemon juice in another bowl and whisk well, pour half of this mixture into a cake pan that matches the drawer of your Ninja dual zone air fryer.
3. Add half of the cocoa mixture you've made in the first step over and spread it, then add the remaining half of the butter mixture, spread it and top with the remaining cocoa mixture.
4. Place the pan in the drawer of your Ninja dual zone air fryer, select BAKE at 180ºC and bake for seventeen mins. leave the cake to cool down, slice and serve.

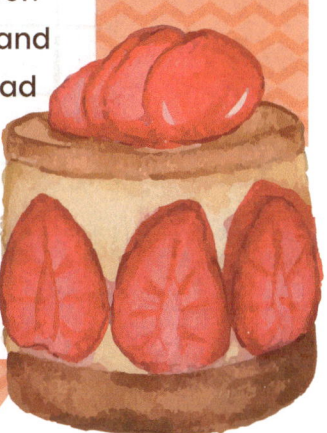

Sponge Cake Recipe

Time: 30 Minutes

Servings: 12

Ingredients

- 750g flour
- 125g Cornflour
- 380ml milk
- 400g sugar
- 5g Bicarbonate of soda
- 250ml olive oil
- 15g baking powder
- 500ml water
- 60ml lemon juice
- 10ml vanilla extract

Directions:

1. Combine Cornflour with flour, Bicarbonate of soda, sugar and baking powder in a bowl and whisk well.
2. Combine the vanilla with milk, oil, water, and lemon juice and whisk
3. Mix both combinations in a third bowl; stir, and transfer to a greased baking dish that matches the drawer of your Ninja dual zone air fryer.
4. Place the pan in the drawer of your Ninja dual zone air fryer, select BAKE at 175°C and bake for twenty mins. leave the cake to cool down, slice and serve.

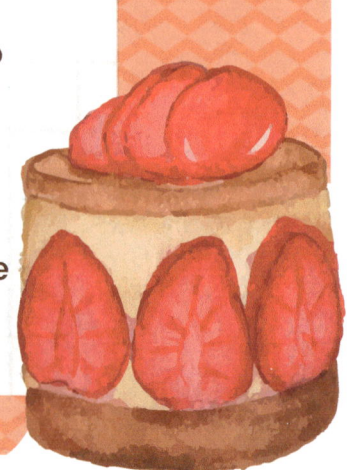

Banana Cake Recipe

Time: 40 Minutes

Servings: 4

Ingredients

- 15g soft butter
- 5g baking powder
- 250g white flour
- 3g cinnamon powder
- 30g honey
- A peeled and mashed banana
- An egg
- 80g Light brown sugar
- Cooking spray

Directions:

1. Use the cooking spray to grease a cake pan that matches the drawer of your Ninja dual zone air fryer and leave it aside.
2. Combine all the mentioned ingredients in a bowl and whisk.
3. Pour the mixture into the greased pan, place the pan in the drawer of your Ninja dual zone air fryer, select BAKE at 175°C and cook for thirty mins. let it cool down, slice and serve.

Plum Cake Recipe

Time: 1 h 20 Mins

Servings: 8

Ingredients

- 800g plums; pitted and cut into quarters
- 30g butter; soft
- 80ml warm milk
- A whisked egg
- A package of dried yeast
- 200g flour
- 75g sugar
- Grated zest of one lemon
- 30g almond flakes

Directions:

1. Combine butter with yeast, three tbsp of sugar, and flour in a bowl and stir well, then add egg with the milk and whisk for around four mins until you obtain a dough.
2. Arrange the dough in a springform pan that matches the drawer of your Ninja dual zone air fryer after greasing it with some butter, cover, and leave aside for 60 mins. Add plumps on top of the butter, and sprinkle the remaining sugar.
3. Place the pan in the drawer of your Ninja dual zone air fryer, select BAKE at 175 °C and bake for thirty-six mins.
4. When it's completed, let it cool down and top with almond flakes & lemon zest. Enjoy!

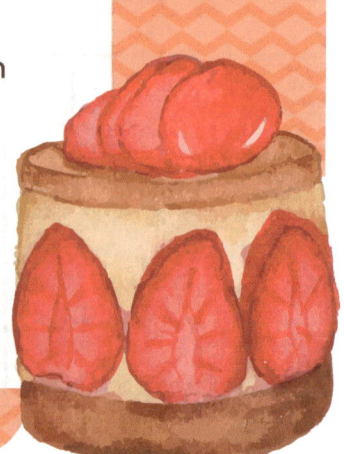

© All rights reserved

Manufactured by Amazon.ca
Bolton, ON

28341371R00057